Pebble® Plus
Bilingüe/ Bilingual

Comida sana con MiPirámide/Healthy Eating with MyPyramid
El agua potable/Drinking Water

por/by Mari C. Schuh

Traducción/Translation: Dr. Martín Luis Guzmán Ferrer
Editor Consultor/Consulting Editor: Dra. Gail Saunders-Smith

Consultor/Consultant: Barbara J. Rolls, PhD
Guthrie Chair in Nutrition
The Pennsylvania State University
University Park, Pennsylvania

Capstone
press®
Mankato, Minnesota

Pebble Plus is published by Capstone Press,
151 Good Counsel Drive, P.O. Box 669, Mankato, Minnesota 56002.
www.capstonepress.com

1 2 3 4 5 6 11 10 09 08 07 06

Library of Congress Cataloging-in-Publication Data
Schuh, Mari C., 1975–
    [Drinking water. English & Spanish]
    El agua potable/de Mari C. Schuh = Drinking water/by Mari C. Schuh.
    p. cm.—(Comida sana con MiPirámide = Healthy eating with MyPyramid)
    Bilingual book with Spanish and English text.
    Includes index.
    ISBN-13: 978-0-7368-6670-5 (hardcover)
    ISBN-10: 0-7368-6670-1 (hardcover)
    1. Water in the body—Juvenile literature. 2. Water—Metabolism—Juvenile literature. 3. Thirst—Juvenile
literature. I. Title.
QP535.H1S3818 2007
613.2'87—dc22
                                     2005037334

Summary: Simple text and photographs describe the importance of drinking water, why your body needs
    water, and ways to enjoy water—in both English and Spanish.

Credits
Katy Kudela, bilingual editor; Eida del Risco, Spanish copy editor; Jennifer Bergstrom, designer;
    Kelly Garvin, photo researcher; Stacy Foster, photo shoot coordinator

Photo Credits
Capstone Press/Karon Dubke, cover, 1, 5, 7, 10–11, 13, 15, 16–17, 19
Corbis/Ariel Skelley, 21; Duomo, 8–9

**The U.S. Department of Agriculture (USDA) does not endorse any products, services,
or organizations.**

Note to Parents and Teachers

The Comida sana con MiPirámide/Healthy Eating with MyPyramid set supports national
science standards related to nutrition and physical health. This book describes drinking
water in both English and Spanish. The images support early readers in understanding the
text. The repetition of words and phrases helps early readers learn new words. This book
also introduces early readers to subject-specific vocabulary words, which are defined in
the Glossary section. Early readers may need assistance to read some words and to use the
Table of Contents, Glossary, Internet Sites, and Index sections of the book.

Table of Contents

Water and Your Body 4

When You Need Water 12

Enjoying Water 16

Glossary 22

Index 24

Internet Sites 24

Tabla de contenidos

El agua y tu cuerpo 4

Cuándo necesitas agua 12

Cómo disfrutar del agua 16

Glosario 23

Índice 24

Sitios de Internet 24

Water and Your Body

Are you thirsty?

Did you drink

lots of water today?

El agua y tu cuerpo

¿Tienes sed?

¿Tomaste mucha

agua hoy?

4

Most of your body
is made of water.
Your body needs water
every day.

La mayor parte de tu
cuerpo está hecho de agua.
Tu cuerpo necesita agua
todos los días.

Everything your body
does on the inside
depends on water.
Water helps all your
body parts work right.

Todo lo que tu cuerpo hace
por adentro depende del agua.
El agua ayuda a todas las partes
de tu cuerpo a funcionar bien.

Your body needs water
to help digest food.
Water also helps your body
get rid of waste.

Tu cuerpo necesita agua para
digerir los alimentos. El agua
también ayuda al cuerpo
a eliminar los desechos.

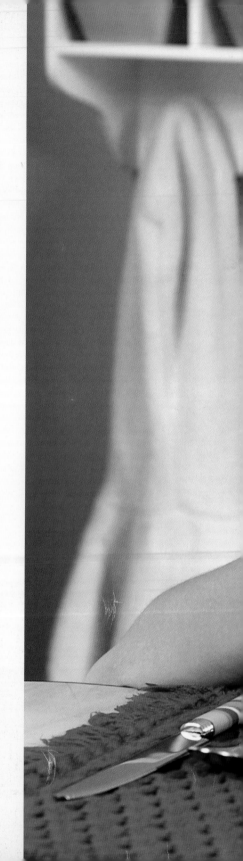

When You Need Water

You lose water

when you play and sweat.

Take water breaks.

Gulp, gulp, gulp.

Cuándo necesitas agua

Pierdes agua cuando juegas

y sudas. Haz pausas para

beber agua. Glu, glu, glu.

Drink plenty of water
when you're sick.
If your body doesn't
have enough water,
it won't work its best.

Cuando estés enfermo toma
mucha agua. Si tu cuerpo no
tiene suficiente agua,
no va a funcionar bien.

Enjoying Water

You can bring water

wherever you go.

Bring bottles of water

along to the park.

Cómo disfrutar del agua

Puedes llevar agua a

cualquier parte que

vayas. Lleva botellas

de agua al parque.

You can get some water
from the food you eat.
Soup, fruits, and vegetables
have lots of water. Enjoy!

Algunos alimentos te dan agua.
La sopa, las frutas y las verduras
tienen muchísima agua. ¡Disfrútalas!

You feel good when you
drink enough water.
Now it's time to play!

Cuando tomas bastante
agua te sientes muy bien.
¡Ahora vamos a jugar!

Glossary

digest—to break down food so it can be absorbed into your blood and used by your body

sweat—having a salty liquid come out through the pores in your skin because you are hot or nervous

thirsty—needing or wanting water or another liquid

waste—food and water that your body does not use or need after food has been digested

Glosario

los desechos—alimentos y agua que tu cuerpo no necesita después de que has digerido la comida

digerir—separar el contenido de los alimentos para que puedan absorberse en la sangre y ser usados por el cuerpo

la sed—necesidad o deseo de agua u otro líquido

el sudor—líquido salino que sale por los poros de la piel porque tienes calor o estas nervioso

Index

body, 6, 8, 10, 14

bottled water, 16

digest, 10

food, 10, 18

park, 16

play, 12, 20

sick, 14

sweat, 12

waste, 10

Internet Sites

FactHound offers a safe, fun way to find Internet sites related to this book. All of the sites on FactHound have been researched by our staff.

Here's how:

1. Visit *www.facthound.com*

2. Choose your grade level.

3. Type in this book ID **0736866701** for age-appropriate sites. You may also browse subjects by clicking on letters, or by clicking on pictures and words.

4. Click on the **Fetch It** button.

FactHound will fetch the best sites for you!

Índice

alimentos, 10, 18

botellas de agua, 16

cuerpo, 6, 8, 10, 14

desechos, 10

digerir, 10

enfermo, 14

jugar, 12, 20

parque, 16

sudas, 12

Sitios de Internet

FactHound proporciona una manera divertida y segura de encontrar sitios de Internet relacionados con este libro. Nuestro personal ha investigado todos los sitios de FactHound. Es posible que los sitios no estén en español.

Se hace así:

1. Visita *www.facthound.com*

2. Elige tu grado escolar.

3. Introduce este código especial **0736866701** para ver sitios apropiados según tu edad, o usa una palabra relacionada con este libro para hacer una búsqueda general.

4. Haz clic en el botón **Fetch It**.

¡FactHound buscará los mejores sitios para ti!